To parents and teachers

We hope you and the children will enjoy reading this story in either English or French. The story is simple, but not *simplified,* so the language of the French and the English is quite natural, although there is lots of repetition.

At the back of the book is a small picture dictionary with the key words and how to pronounce them. There is also a simple pronunciation guide to the whole story on the last page.

Here are a few suggestions on using the book:

- Read the story aloud in English first, to get to know it. Treat it like any other picture book: look at the pictures, talk about the story and the characters, and so on.

- Then look at the picture dictionary and say the French names for the key words. Ask the children to repeat them. Concentrate on speaking the words out loud, rather than reading them.

- Go back and read the story again, this time in English *and* French. Don't worry if your pronunciation isn't quite correct. Just have fun trying it out. Check the guide at the back of the book, if necessary, but you'll soon pick up how to say the French words.

- When you think you and the children are ready, you can try reading the story in French only. Ask the children to say it with you. Ask them to read it only if they are eager to try. The spelling could be confusing and put them off.

- Above all, encourage the children to try it, and give lots of praise. Little children are usually quite unself-conscious and this is excellent for building up confidence in a foreign language.

First edition for the United States, its dependencies, Canada, and the Philippines published in 2006 by Barron's Educational Series, Inc. Text and illustrations © Copyright 2005 by *b small publishing*

All rights reserved. No part of this book may be reproduced in any form, by photostat, microfilm, xerography, or any other means, or incorporated into any information retrieval system, electronic or mechanical, without the written permission of the copyright owner.

Address all inquiries to:
Barron's Educational Series, Inc. • 250 Wireless Boulevard • Hauppauge, New York 11788 • **http://www.barronseduc.com**

ISBN-13: 978-0-7641-5876-6   ISBN-10: 0-7641-5876-7
Library of Congress Catalog Card Number 2005921557

Printed in China
9 8 7 6 5 4 3 2 1

Space postman

Le facteur spatial

Lone Morton

Pictures by Martin Ursell
French by Marie-Thérèse Bougard

BARRON'S

Captain Crater climbs
into his spaceship.
He is the space postman.

Le capitaine Crater monte
dans son engin spatial.
Il est facteur spatial.

He turns the blue dial to the left
Il tourne la manette bleue à gauche

and the yellow dial to the right.
et la manette jaune à droite.

He presses the green button:
Il appuie sur le bouton vert:

GO!
PARTEZ!

BLAST OFF!

C'EST LE LANCEMENT!

Whoosh! He takes off into the sky.

Zoum! Il s'en va dans le ciel.

His first stop is Planet Fizz.
He has a letter for Princess Shush.

Son premier arrêt est la planète Fizz.
Il a une lettre pour la Princesse Shush.

It's an invitation to a wedding.
She is very happy.

C'est une invitation à un mariage.
Elle est très contente.

Second stop: Planet Ooloo.
He has a package for Farmer Flop.

Deuxième arrêt: la planète Oulou.
Il a un colis pour Flop, le fermier.

It's a big book.
He is very happy.

C'est un grand livre.
Il est très content.

The next stop is Planet Astro.
He has a postcard for Blop.

Le prochain arrêt est la planète Astro.
Il a une carte postale pour Blop.

Oh, no!
Oh, non!

On the way, the door opens…
En route la porte s'ouvre…

…and the mailbag falls out!
…et le sac postal tombe!

Captain Crater lands on Planet Astro.
But there is no mailbag.

Le capitaine Crater se pose
sur la planète Astro.
Mais il n'y a pas de sac postal.

"I am going to look for it," he says to Blop. "But I will come back."

"Je vais aller le chercher", dit-il à Blop. "Mais je reviens".

He flies east.
Il va à l'est.

He flies west.
Il va à l'ouest.

He flies north and then south.
Il va au nord et puis au sud.

But he can't find the mailbag anywhere.

Mais il ne trouve le sac postal nulle part.

"Bleep, bleep, bleep," his phone rings.

"Blip, blip, blip", son téléphone sonne.

"Hello, hello. It's the space police.
We have found a mailbag...

"Allô, allô. C'est la police spatiale.
Nous avons trouvé un sac postal...

...hanging from a star!"

...accroché à une étoile"!

Captain Crater is very happy.

Le capitaine Crater est très content.

Blop's postcard is from his twin brother, Blip.

La carte postale de Blop vient de son frère jumeau, Blip.

"He's arriving tomorrow on the Space Bus!"
Blop is very happy.

"Il arrive demain par le bus spatial"!
Blop est très content.

Pronouncing French

Don't worry if your pronunciation isn't quite correct.
The important thing is to be willing to try. The pronunciation
guide here will help but it cannot be completely accurate:

• Read the guide as naturally as possible, as if it were English.

• Put stress on the letters in *italics*, as in fak-*ter*.

If you can, ask a French person to help, and move on as soon as
possible to speaking the words without the guide.

Note: French adjectives usually have two forms, one for masculine
and one for feminine nouns, as in **content** and **contente.**

Words Les mots

leh moh

star

l'étoile

let*w*al

sky

le ciel

leh see-*el*

space bus

le bus spatial

leh boos spah-see-*al*

spaceship

l'engin spatial

lon*jah* spah-see-*al*

postman
le facteur
leh fak-*ter*

mailbag
le sac postal
leh sak post*al*

postcard
la carte postal
lah kart post*al*

happy
content,
contente
kon*tah*, kon*tant*

package
le colis
leh ko*lee*

letter
la lettre
lah letr'

big
grand, grande
groh, grond

book
le livre
leh leevr'

north

nord
nor

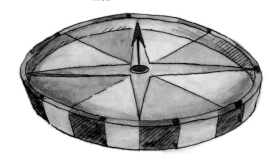

west

ouest
oowest

east

est
est

south

sud
sood

left

gauche
gohsh

right

droite
drwat

blue

bleu, bleue
bluh, bluh

yellow

jaune
zhown

green

vert, verte
vair, vairt

A simple guide to pronouncing this French story

Le facteur spatial
leh fak-*ter* spah-see-*al*

Le capitaine Crater monte dans son engin spatial.
leh kapee-*ten* krat-*air* mont dah soh an*jah* spah-see-*al*

Il est facteur spatial.
eel eh fak-*ter* spah-see-*al*

Il tourne la manette bleue à gauche
eel toorn lah ma*net* bluh ah gohsh

et la manette jaune à droite.
eh lah ma*net* zhown ah drwat

Il appuie sur le bouton vert:
eel ap*wee* syoor leh boo*tah* vair

PARTEZ!
par-*teh*

C'EST LE LANCEMENT!
seh leh lans-*mah*

Zoum! Il s'en va dans le ciel.
zoom, eel soh va dah leh see-*el*

Son premier arrêt est la planète Fizz.
soh premee-*eh* a*reh* teh lah pla*net* feez

Il a une lettre pour la Princesse Shush.
eel ah yoon letr' poor lah prah-*sess* shoosh

C'est une invitation à un mariage.
seh toon ahn-vee-tah-see-*oh* ah ahn maree-*aj*

Elle est très contente.
el eh treh kon*tant*

Deuxième arrêt: la planète Oulou.
deh-zee-*em* a*reh* lah pla*net* ooloo

Il a un colis pour Flop, le fermier.
eel ah ahn ko*lee* poor flop, leh fairm-ee-*eh*

C'est un grand livre.
set ahn grah leevr'

Il est très content.
eel eh treh kon*tah*

Le prochain arrêt est la planète Astro.
leh pro*shahn* a*reh* eh lah pla*net* astro

Il a une carte postale pour Blop.
eel ah yoon kart pos*tal* poor blop

Oh, non! En route, la porte s'ouvre…
oh noh, ahn root, lah port soovr'

…et le sac postal tombe!
eh leh sak pos*tal* tomb

Le capitaine Crater se pose
leh kapee-*ten* krat-*air* seh pose

sur la planète Astro.
soor lah pla*net* astro

Mais il n'y a pas de sac postal.
meh eel nee ah pah deh sak pos*tal*

"Je vais aller le chercher", dit-il à Blop.
zher vayz a*leh* leh shair-*sheh* deet-eel ah blop

"Mais je reviens".
meh zheh reh-vee*ah*

Il va à l'est. Il va à l'ouest.
eel vah ah lest, eel va ah loo*west*

Il va au nord et puis au sud.
eel va oh nor, eh pwee oh sood

Mais il ne trouve le sac postal
meh eel nuh troov pah leh sak pos*tal*

nulle part.
nool pah

"Blip, blip, blip", son téléphone sonne.
bleep, bleep, bleep, soh teh-leh-*fohn* son

"Allô, allô. C'est la police spatiale.
allo, allo, seh lah po*lees* spah-see-*al*

Nous avons trouvé un sac postal…
noo za*voh* troo*veh* ahn sak pos*tal*

…accroché à une étoile"!
…akro*sheh* ah oon et-*wal*

Le capitaine Crater est très content.
ler kapee-*ten* krat-*air* eh treh kon*toh*

La carte postale de Blop
lah kart pos*tal* der blop

vient de son frère jumeau, Blip.
vee-*ah* deh soh frair zhoo*moh* bleep

"Il arrive demain par le bus spatial"!
eel a*reev* deh-mah par leh boos spah-see-*al*

Blop est très content.
blop eh treh kon*toh*